THE

POWER

OF UNITY

Charles Fillmore's

Amazing Discoveries

THE POWER

OF UNITY

Charles Fillmore's

Amazing Discoveries

Ruth L. Miller

illustrated by Martha Shonkwiler

A *Paths of Power* book

from

WISEWOMAN PRESS

The Power of Unity: Charles Fillmore's Amazing Discoveries

By Ruth L. Miller
Illustrations by Martha Shonkwiler

WiseWoman Press
Portland, OR 97217

www.wisewomanpress.com

ISBN: 978-0-945385-19-6

Appreciation to Unity Institute and the Unity Association for sharing video and photographic material

Imagine growing up with Indians as your neighbors and playmates—then having your father leave, then getting seriously injured so you can't play anymore....

Imagine completing your education at a neighbor's kitchen table at night, while working as a printer's helper during the day—even though your leg still hurts and is shorter than the other one...

Imagine getting a job with the railroad and moving to the Wild West, then meeting the love of your life— only to have her move away!

Imagine driving a mule train over the mountains into the mining fields, with one leg lame ... building a business and then losing it ... marrying the love of your life and then watching her get sicker and sicker... and then miraculously healed!

That's how life was when a Power stronger than anyone led Charles to heal that leg and then help millions of others to experience that same Power!

CONTENTS

I. Beginnings

Way up in the North woods of Minnesota, back in the 1850s, a boy named Charles lived with his parents and brother.

His father was a trapper and trader with the native Chippewas, so when Charles was very young, he played with the children among the lodges of the native people. He even learned a few words in the Chippewa language.

One day, when he was little more than a baby, a chief rode up and grabbed Charles out of his mother's arms—returning him perfectly well that night. What happened during those long anxious hours was never discussed, but it may have contributed to Charles' experiences later in life.

As Charles grew older, his father was often gone, earning money for the family by trapping furs in Canada. So it was up to Charles and his brother to do the daily chores that made it possible for their mother to cook and clean.

They chopped the wood for the "monster" fireplace that kept their cabin warm during the long, below-zero winters. They also gathered nuts and berries, caught fish in the river, and made sure the water was drawn from the well. And during the winter, they brought up each day's food from the root cellar where it was stored.

Finally, when Charles was seven, his father left for good. He moved a few miles away, living alone in a cabin and leaving his wife to the protection of his young   sons.

One cold winter's day when he was 10 years old, Charles was ice-skating and fell. By the time he was out of the water, his leg was broken and his hip was badly damaged.

The nearest doctor was miles away and the wound became infected before it was properly set. Things went rapidly from bad to worse, and Charles was stuck in bed for months while the infection was treated.

Every few weeks a different doctor would come and try a new technique, and in later years Charles would say that "each one wondered how I survived the treatment of the 'quack' that had preceded him."

The infection seemed to take over his body. He was often on the edge of death, with his mother keeping watch beside him, bringing him cold cloths for his fever and trying to coax him to drink a little broth.

It was months before Charles could walk at all, and it turned out that the injured leg had stopped growing while he was ill, so he needed crutches and a 4-inch block of wood on his shoe to make up for the difference in length between his two legs. And for years he limped badly because his hip hurt so much when it was forced to move.

Suddenly, this active, curious boy was limited to reading, writing, and watching others. There was little else he could do to fill the long days. There was no such thing as tv, radio, or computers, and books were scarce. Playing with the other boys and helping his mother with the hard work of caring for their home were no longer possible. On top of that, he had gotten way behind in school!

At first, it was hard to be still after having been so active. Charles read everything in sight and did all the lessons that his teacher sent home with his brother, but life was still pretty boring—and frustrating! He wanted to be outdoors! He wanted to

visit the Indians he'd met with his father! He wanted
to be with other people! He wanted to be doing
things!

Finally the day came when he was strong enough
to go back to school. Then, almost immediately, his
brother left. Charles and his mother, who had been
through so much together while he was ill, were on
their own.

As Charles saw it, school was no longer an
option. Although his mother earned a little as a
dressmaker for the women who had moved into the
area, he realized he had to earn some money if the
two of them were going to make it.

He convinced a local printer to take him on as a
"printer's devil." He did odd jobs around the printing
plant in return for a small wage and the opportunity
to learn the trade.

It was difficult for him, at first—especially with his injured leg—but he soon began to enjoy the work, as well as the income he could take home to his mother.

Printing presses and the printing process hadn't changed much since they were invented almost 400 years earlier, so Charles was learning pretty much the same things that Benjamin Franklin had learned in Boston and London, almost 200 years before!

As a "printer's devil" Charles learned all the tricks of the trade. His curiosity drove him to observe everything and to ask all kinds of questions. He learned how to set the paper into the press and crank the big handle, applying just the right amount of pressure to ensure that the ink that had been spread across the letter blocks would leave an impression without smearing.

He also learned how to set the letter blocks into their racks, spacing them just right to fit the margins on the page. He learned how to cut the paper into "folios," little "mini-books" of 32 pages that would be stitched together into the actual books and bound at a bindery. He also learned how to figure how much a job would cost and how to ship the product to the customer. And he got to read everything they printed! It was fascinating!

But working with the printer, learning to set the "type," or letters to be printed on the big press, and checking, or "proofing," the pages for errors, made him very aware of how far behind he was in grammar and spelling. He struggled hard to get things right.

Then, a neighbor made an offer. She was home-schooling her son and knew her boy would do better if he had someone to work with. Would Charles be willing to join them? He could help a little around her house in return for the lessons and they could meet when he wasn't needed at the printing plant.

It was the perfect solution! His friend's mother was one of the very few women at that time with a teaching degree. She had graduated from the 2-year teacher's program at Oberlin College, and she knew just how to keep these boys aware, interested, and enthusiastic.

She taught them about nature and the classics: poetry, history, and legends from the ancient Greeks and Romans, making those ancient heroes part of their dreams. Then she introduced them to

Shakespeare, and helped them bring the characters alive by speaking those rhyming verses aloud. More poetry and essays from the modern American Transcendentalist writers, including Ralph Waldo Emerson, Walt Whitman, and Henry David Thoreau, rounded out their literary education. Charles loved the way those men talked about the glories of Nature!

She also taught them mathematics: algebra, geometry, and just enough trigonometry so they could figure out how to build a building.

Then she introduced them to the biology, chemistry, and physics of the day—starting an interest in science that lasted the rest of Charles' life.

Charles and his friend worked together at the kitchen table and often pushed each other to do better.

During those years, Charles moved on from the printing plant to work in the local grocery store and then the bank, each time learning all he could about the business as well as the job. He learned how to keep accounts and to manage cash—and about the importance of maintaining good credit.

All the energy that Charles had once put into his sports and hunting, he now put into his studies, his jobs, and strengthening his injured and shrunken leg. They were long days, beginning at dawn with the chores to help his mother and ending with late nights of studying, but he enjoyed them—even as he began to dream of the life that he would build for himself.

II. Learning to Get By

The time came when Charles felt that he had learned all that he could in Minnesota. He was barely earning enough to support his mother and him, and there was no room for advancement with the businesses in town. More importantly, his study partner had gone on to join the military, so Charles had no one to explore new ideas with. He decided to move on.

The Train to Texas

While Charles was growing up, the railroad was being built across North America and the word went out, "go West, young man!"

So in 1874, drawn by tales of the booming West, 20-year-old Charles left Minnesota to make his way in the world. He boarded the train and left his mother in St. Cloud with a promise to send her his wages and to bring her to live with him as soon as he settled.

He found his way to Dennison, Texas, and took a job at the local railroad station, counting the freight as

it was loaded and unloaded, and, again, learning all
he could about the business as well as his job.

He learned so well that when his supervisor took
ill, Charles was the only one who knew enough to
take over, and soon he was promoted from freight-
counter to cashier. His job was to sell people their
tickets and take the payments for shipping the
packages and larger shipments that went through his
station. He had learned how to do most of this kind
of work in his jobs in St. Cloud, so, once he had a
system figured out, it was easy work and left him
with time to explore and learn.

Charles sent for his mother as promised, and the
two shared a home once again.

Charles was a young man with an inquiring
mind. Like most young men of the day, he had spent
a fair amount of time at the local tavern, acquiring a
taste for whiskey and beer. Unlike most of them,
though, he really appreciated a good book and a
lively discussion about ideas.

So Charles was drawn to attend lectures and
public meetings. Some of these were book groups,
which were called back then "literary societies,"
where people would meet, read essays, passages of
novels, and poetry aloud, and discuss their meaning
and impact on their lives and thinking.

Another form of entertainment that was
becoming popular in the years Charles was growing
up was the "tent meeting." Many of these were
"revival" meetings, in which preachers who traveled
from town to town would use all kinds of methods to

convince people to revive their faith in Christ and "give up their sinful ways."

Some of these tent meetings were focused on specific issues, like giving up alcohol. They were called "temperance meetings," and were often led by women.

All of these meetings included testimonials and readings by people in the crowd.

It was at one such meeting that Charles made a discovery that would set the course of his life.

Meeting an Amazing Woman

She was about 26 and he was barely 20, but he knew, the moment he heard her voice, that the lovely redhead would be his wife. In fact, he heard a small voice inside say, "There's your wife, Charles."

She was reading poetry aloud, and something in her voice and in her understanding of what she read connected with his own inquiring mind. She had spirit as well as intellect, and was so lovely that she took his breath away.

Her name was Mary Caroline, but everyone called her Myrtle. She was a teacher, working part time at a school in Texas as she tried to heal a respiratory problem she'd been told she'd inherited and would ultimately kill her. Like the woman who had tutored him in Minnesota, she had graduated from the "literary course" at Oberlin College in Ohio, and was familiar with many of the books he had read back home.

Myrtle was raised in Paigetown, Ohio, a small country town that her father had founded on farm land at an intersection. Always a frail child, she loved to read, and spent hours sitting by a little stream communing with God.

From her earliest days as a teacher, Myrtle was loved for her sweet disposition, respect and appreciation for her students, and love of learning.

Charles was in love for life.

He made it a point to participate in every group event she attended: fossil hunts, river excursions, bird-watching hikes. Even though his injured leg made every step an effort, it was worth it to be with her and to explore the many ideas and possibilities they shared in common.

Then, in 1878, she returned to Missouri and resumed her teaching career. Charles was sad, but saw it as an opportunity to work hard and earn some money to create a home.

He started writing letters to her, which, happily, she responded to, and they continued to share many dreams and ideas through the mail.

In The Mines

Soon after Myrtle left, Charles took his savings from the Texas job, hired out as a mule-team driver, and made his way across the Rocky Mountains to the silver mining boom in Colorado, hoping to earn enough to be able to support her.

In spite of being only medium-build and lame, Charles handled the mules well. The days were long and hot, and the nights were cold. Charles would hang tarps around the wagon frame, keeping the warmth in so he could sleep under it. Riding in the seat of the wagon, he managed those mules up and down the narrow trails along the steep sides of the mountain passes.

Only once did he lose his team—on one of those long, steep descents, when the mules got going too fast to make it around the curve. Then he, like many a driver before him, leapt off the wagon just before it went over the edge, mules and all.

In the face of such constant danger, Charles decided that if he was going to live a full life, he'd better try something different. Drawing on the love of science he had gained from his studies with his neighbor, he went to a local school and learned enough about minerals to become an assayer. His new job was to weigh the ore the miners brought in and tell them how much gold was in it.

He built a partnership with another man, rented space in a barn-like building made of loosely attached boards, and the two did well together.

In the evenings, after the day's work was done, Charles wrote frequent, long letters to Myrtle, continuing the kind of conversations they'd had in Texas. He wrote about the natural world around him, about the miners and their activities, and he shared his thoughts about the nature of the world and of God. She replied in kind, and his love for her remained strong.

Finally, after almost 2 years, he believed he had established himself well enough to support a wife.

III. Married life

As soon as Charles felt he had something to offer a wife, he wrote his intentions to Myrtle.

She accepted his proposal in a lovely, loving letter, and he traveled to her brother's home in Clinton, Missouri, where they were married in March

of 1881.

The newlyweds then rode immediately off to Charles' new home in Gunnison, Colorado (much to her students' distress, for they truly loved their pretty teacher!). They took a carriage to the train station, rode the coal-fired train across the plains, then took a stage coach across the mountains until the trail gave out. It was early in the season, so they rode in a horse-drawn sleigh for a while, then trudged through ice and snow for the last stretch of the trip. So much for a honeymoon!

Dealing with Disruption

Unfortunately, the mining boom that Charles had been profiting from in Gunnison turned almost immediately to bust and the newly married couple had to leave their home just a few months after they arrived—not just their home, but all the property and other assets that Charles had acquired in his new business.

They moved back across the mountains, to Pueblo, Colorado, that summer, arriving with a wagon full of household goods and books—and a dime.

Charles knew he had to find a home and food for his wife, immediately. He found a room for rent and left Myrtle there to unpack. Then he went to the grocery store and arranged to have a few essentials delivered to her, "C.O.D." which means "cash on delivery."

With a dime in his pocket, he made his way through the streets of Pueblo, to discover what might be possible.

Soon, he met an old friend. Charles persuaded the man to lend him $10, which he then took back to the grocery store. There he found the groceries he had ordered, which had been returned for lack of payment. With a look of great surprise, he pulled the $10 bill out of his pocket as if nothing could be further from the truth.

While the grocer was counting out the change, Charles went even further. He suggested that perhaps the vacant space at the back of the store might be available for him to rent as an office.

He left that store with a home, food, and an office space.

Making a Family

Charles was once more successful. He had discovered in Gunnison that he had an uncanny ability to put together real estate deals. The habit of working long days that he had learned in Minnesota, combined with his determination to learn everything he could about the place, its people, and its potential, brought them quickly into the mainstream of the community.

Myrtle was active with the Episcopal church, where she taught and sang, and Charles built a very successful partnership, buying and selling land and buildings with Charles Small.[1] They had a nice home, were able to bring Charles' mother to live with them, and their first two sons, Lowell Page (named after their favorite poet, James Russell Lowell) and Waldo Rickert (named after Ralph Waldo Emerson and a cousin), were born during those years.

The only sad part of their time in Pueblo was that Myrtle's health steadily worsened, but they made the best of it. They spent time taking walks and picnics in Nature, and met with people of like minds to read interesting books and poetry, as they had when they first met. The local doctor was helpful and kind, but let them know that Myrtle's days were limited.

Then the real estate boom in Pueblo came to an abrupt end, leaving them nearly bankrupt, once again. The property they owned was worth next to nothing and there was no way to earn an income in those depressed times.

When they took stock of their situation, Charles and Myrtle decided to move to another growing town, Kansas City, Missouri. It wasn't far from Myrtle's family and was growing rapidly, which looked good. But most important, it was much more stable, making it an ideal place for them to start over.

---

[1] Charles Small later married one of the Brooks sisters and helped to create the College and Church of Divine Science in Denver.

IV. Miracles in Kansas City

The strain of moving, with the added stress of financial difficulties, was really hard on Myrtle's health. By 1888 the doctors had diagnosed her illness as tuberculosis (TB) and were giving up on her, suggesting that she would no longer be among the living in a matter of months.

Of course this was unacceptable to them both, but they didn't see what they could do about it. Myrtle took all the medications the doctors gave her, rested often, and prayed hard. It helped a lot when Charles' mother arrived to help keep the household going.

They went about their daily routines, caring for their sons, creating a new home, and building Charles' new business. And, when Myrtle was up to it, they still attended poetry readings and lectures. They were particularly interested whenever someone came to town to talk about new ideas or developments in science.

It was at one such lecture that their lives were changed completely.

The man's name was E. B. Weeks and he had just graduated from a school in Chicago, run by a woman named Emma Curtis Hopkins. His lectures were based on her lessons, and held very unusual ideas about who we are, what God is, and how we experience health or illness.

Mr. Weeks said one sentence in particular that got Myrtle's attention: "I am a child of God; therefore I do not inherit illness."

All her life Myrtle had been told that she'd *inherited* TB and it would kill her. She'd also been taught that God was a distant, judging figure, more concerned about her sins than her wellbeing. Now, for the first time, she saw a different possibility.

So, for the next weeks and months, she spent as much time as she could studying her Bible. She focused particularly on the many passages in which God and Jesus promise a full, healthy, satisfying life. After reading for a while, she would close her eyes and *feel* the presence of the Holy Spirit, the Comforter, in her life, and *know* the love of her divine Father in Heaven, whose will is to be done on Earth.

After 2 weeks, friends noticed a difference. After 2 months, they started studying and praying with her. And after 2 years, she was completely free of all symptoms, and never experienced them again.

"I am a Child of God therefore..."

Charles was delighted—and impressed! He had never had much interest in church, though he supported Myrtle's involvement. He just didn't see that what the preachers had to say was all that meaningful—after all, he felt, Nature was sacred enough.

But seeing his own wife use her religious faith to heal her body—now that was worth paying attention to!

Charles went about this new interest as he had each one before. He immediately started to study every religious book he could find, along with the Bible. Translations of sacred texts from India and Persia had recently been printed in the U.S. and numerous British and American writers had written about God and humanity and healing, over the years.

Charles read them all: the *Baghavad Gita,* the *Zend-Avesta,* the *Upanishads,* the *Tao Te Ching,* the *Koran,* as well as the New and Old Testament, his favorites, Emerson and Alcott, and some European writers, like Goethe and Swedenborg. He even read the Christian Science literature, like *Life and Health with Key to the Scriptures,* by Mary Baker Eddy.

He wanted to know who and what God is and how healing happened. But what he found was what he later called "a mess of contradictions."

So Charles decided to "go to headquarters." He figured that if God was real God could be communicated with, "or the whole thing was a fraud."

He set aside about an hour each evening, after work was done and his sons were in bed, to sit in silence and wait for God to speak to him.

Needless to say, he didn't hear much. For almost a year he sat and waited, and as he went through the last few weeks, he was thinking about giving up.

Helpful Guidance

It was a difficult year. Kansas City had stopped growing. Real estate was no longer worth anything, and once more, Charles was facing bankruptcy.

He was considering returning to Colorado, trying in another boom town.

Then he had a dream. In it, he realized it was not the first time he'd dreamt this. Someone was guiding him up and down the streets of Kansas City, showing him familiar places, and saying he "had a work to do here." And that "the invisible power that has located you here will continue to be with you and aid you…"

Reflecting on this, and looking over the past few months, he realized that he felt better in general, and that his hip was healing. More, he realized he was having frequent dreams that helped him at home and at work.

He decided that his time "in the silence" was getting results, so he continued the practice, feeling grateful for what was happening.

Accepting the Power

Soon he started to be aware of a still pool of wisdom, ready to overflow into his awareness. Later, he called it a deep reservoir, out of which each of us is a stream, flowing just as full as we allow.

As he "listened" to this inner wisdom, he received guidance on business and personal matters and began to feel a youthful joy and enthusiasm that he had lost when focusing on the problems of keeping his business and family going.

More than that, he noticed that the signs of aging were reversing: his weak eye was better, and the hearing was returning to his right ear. Then he saw that his leg wasn't as stiff as it had been—and then, over the next months and years, he noticed it was getting longer, and the strange, tight scar-tissue skin was actually transforming into living flesh!

Soon Charles was joining Myrtle and her friends each evening for prayer. They talked about people they knew or who had written to them about problems and then sat silently, each connecting with the divine Power in their own way. In a few days, they were hearing from the people that they'd been praying with and for that the problems were gone, or at least greatly diminished!

Charles got the idea of sharing their new understandings in a magazine—he knew a local printer and still remembered enough about the printing business to do that!

So the little group started printing and sending out a few pages each month, which they called *Modern Thought*. It was more like what we would call, today, a newsletter, but it was a way to share their understanding and to invite others to participate with them.

In the meantime, Charles continued to work in real estate to support his growing boys and this new venture.

Silent Help

Charles and Myrtle realized that if their prayer work for people who'd written them worked, then anyone, anywhere, could help anyone else, anywhere else, through the same kind of prayer.

So they put a little notice in the magazine, inviting others of like mind to join them at 10 o'clock each evening, holding thoughts of wellbeing for those who had written to them while connecting with the Power of God—wherever they were at that time.

The response was immediate and gratifying—lots of people said they'd like to be part of this new process! They did ask, however, that it be at 9 pm instead of 10—those were pretty late hours for farmers and their families who were up before dawn!

So each night Charles and Myrtle, and whoever happened to be in the neighborhood, would say a few words about the people and problems that needed prayer. Then they'd sit together in the silence, knowing that, all across the country, hundreds of others were joining them.

They'd sit and focus their thoughts on God—as Light, Life, Wisdom, Health, Peace, Balance, and Abundant Supply. They would *feel* that divine Power, those qualities, at work in their lives and in the world. And they would sit with those feelings until they felt a completion—until they knew it was done.

At that point they'd feel a deep sense of gratitude for a loving Father-Mother God who nurtured them and answered their prayers. And in that gratitude they'd declare *Amen*, which means "so it is;" "so be it;" or, literally, "on this ground I stand and from henceforth will I have my being."

Over the years to come, this process would become the essence of their work, and millions of letters would come to them requesting prayer support, until they built a team of volunteers working 24-7-365 to address the requests—but that's getting ahead of our story.

V. An Organization Emerges

The people who gathered in Charles' and Myrtle's home decided to form the Society of Silent Help. They rented offices in a building that housed several such groups and had regular meetings, with visiting lecturers, readings from newly discovered books, and lively conversations about the ideas.

After a while, songs and prayers were incorporated into these meetings, until, for some, they were as powerfully inspiring as the best church services.

But Charles was wary of replacing traditional churches. He felt that the processes and studies their group engaged in supported each person's religion, rather than replacing it—and he was very clear about that. This was a school of thought, not a religion.

Part of our purpose in life, as he saw it, was to continue to expand our ideas, and he believed that religion codified and restricted thought. Many years later, well past his 90th birthday, he would say "I still reserve the right to change my mind!"

The first few people who gathered in their living room moved on to other places and ideas, but Charles and Myrtle felt called to continue the work.

In addition to the magazine, Charles started to print little booklets, each one with a favorite article from the magazine or the transcript from a well-received lecture.

The Society

New folks, seeing the magazine or attending a lecture and purchasing pamphlets, wanted to become part of what the Fillmores were doing. And so it became time to find a name for the group.

Charles contemplated names for weeks. Then, one day, in the prayer circle, he had it: *Unity!* "That's what we're about!" he announced (to everyone's amazement, for he didn't usually speak during their time in the silence!). But he was so enthusiastic about having named the power and the process with one word that everyone simply accepted it. And so it was.

Buildings and Books

An organization that has regular meetings and produces a magazine and booklets needs a place to call its own; after a while, living rooms, basements, and shared office spaces just don't work any more. So Charles started using his skills as a real estate developer to create a home for the Society of Unity.

They rented a building, at first; then bought a building on the edge of a residential district. The printing press was in the basement, classrooms and offices were on the upper floors, and they made one floor into a beautiful meeting hall.

In the new space, people were always coming and going. Volunteers would meet to pray, or help with the printing and mailing of materials. Students would attend classes, or come to study in the library. Men and women of all ages were fascinated by these new ideas and wanted to learn more.

Because so many people spent so much time in this wonderful new space, Charles and Myrtle decided to add a cafeteria for lunches. At first, they offered meals for free, as they had at home. They found, though, that people were hesitant to take advantage of this hospitality, so Charles, Myrtle, and the other leaders of the group decided to charge a little (50 cents, when lunch at the local tavern was a dollar) to make people feel better. Second helpings, however, were free—a tradition that lasted almost a hundred years.

And children were not left out. Myrtle still loved to teach, so she set up classes for children, training others to lead them as well. She also put together her own magazine, just for little ones—she called it *Wee Wisdom.*

A Ministry

As the organization grew, Charles and Myrtle were asked again to offer Sunday services. The people who prayed with them and worked with them were finding it hard to go to a church that preached "miserable sinners" and then come to a class that celebrated God as a loving Father whose "good will" was to "give the Kingdom" to his children.

Charles talked with Emma Hopkins, the woman who had taught that first lecturer whose words had transformed their lives. Mrs. Hopkins had come to visit them several times and was a popular lecturer in Kansas City, as well as Chicago and other places. She was one of the few people in the world who had read as widely as Charles, and they delighted in their visits together.

Mrs. Hopkins suggested that Charles and Myrtle come to Chicago and complete the "Advanced Class" which would qualify them for ordination in the seminary she had founded. Then, she said, they could offer church services that were based on "all the Bibles of the world" and not be restricted to one set of ideas, or doctrines, while still teaching the Truth of Christ.

Charles was delighted! His writing and teaching and healing work was more than satisfying, but it had bothered him to see people disturbed by their Sunday morning church experience. Myrtle, too, was glad to find a way to meet these peoples' needs.

So, in December of 1890, the two of them boarded the train again, and spent 10 days in Chicago, with 120 other students, studying Mrs. Hopkins "Advanced Course." Each day they would work through the Bible and other sacred texts and discover how they supported each of Mrs. Hopkins' 12 lessons.

They learned to logically reason out how God, as good, is "omnipresent," which means present everywhere, all the time. They learned how to claim God's good as the only truth, even when things seemed to be difficult or unpleasant. They also learned that God's goodness is "omnipotent," which means all-power, so there can be no other power anywhere. And this means that sickness has no power, poverty has no power, unkind words have no power — none. God is the only power, which is good.

VI. Unfailing Supply

During their time in Chicago, as they came to really understand these ideas, Charles and Myrtle made an important decision, which they wrote down. They vowed never to do anything just for the money, but always to work in service to God and humanity, trusting that all would be provided.

They wrote this vow like a letter and put it away, not to be shared with others, but just as a reminder of their sacred promise. It was fifty years later that it was discovered by others.

They were determined to practice the methods that Jesus taught, and to apply them in every area of their life.

But shifting habits of thought and action can take time. So it took a while for Charles to really accept that he didn't have to earn a living in order to support his spiritual activities. The old habit of trying to make a deal was a hard one to break, until he found a way to channel it into their new work.

They asked for nothing in return for their prayer work, counseling and classes, accepting only what they called "Love Offerings." Sometimes those offerings came in the form of a good suit that could be altered to fit, or a box of toys at Christmas time. And sometimes it seemed there was no way they could make it. But, having made their agreement, they stuck with it, and Charles gave the credit to

Myrtle for keeping him on track when he started to slip into the old way of thinking.

So, for the next fifteen years, Charles and Myrtle raised their sons, wrote and edited articles for their magazines, met with and helped people who sought help or healing, taught classes, and led study groups. Then, every night, they sat in Silent Unity, holding the truth of God's omnipresent goodness with people around the world.

They were good years, and many wonderful things happened. People were healed. Families were restored. The organization grew. Hundreds of people were employed in the Unity work. Dozens of Unity centers were formed in towns and cities across the country.

New buildings were built in Kansas City to house the printing presses as well as the large congregations who met on Sundays and Wednesdays to listen to "Papa Charles" speak and "Mother Myrtle" lead prayers and meditations.

They even acquired a radio station! And, along with the regular daily programs, Charles could be seen in the store-front studio, often at 2 or 3 in the morning, sharing his latest ideas and responding to questions from his listeners.

Parties were held for every possible holiday or celebration, and people would dance and laugh and have a wonderful time, and sometime during the event, Charles would stand up and sing some well-known tune, raising spirits still further.

Then, most nights, Charles would return to his office and finish recording the income and expenditures of the day, or writing letters in response to the many requests for help he received, or editing an article for the next issue of his magazine, now called *Unity*.

He'd usually stay up 'til almost dawn, then catch a couple hours of sleep, rising in time to be dressed and ready for a 9 a.m. meeting.

He made up for the missed sleep by closing his eyes several times during the day and either napping or meditating, depending on the time and place.

Sometimes people would say something in a group, believing he was asleep where he was sitting with his eyes closed in the rocking chair, only to be surprised by his response to their comments later on!

Often, during the summer, the whole family would pack up and head for the mountains of Colorado. There, they would live in tents and Charles would show his boys some of the things he learned growing up in the wild North woods.

As news went out that Charles and Myrtle were in the area, though, people would ask them to teach and pray with them. So, over time, a summer camp program became a regular part of their lives.

And amazingly, though they did nothing for the purpose of getting money, there was always enough: enough food to go around; enough clothing to wear and share; enough paper and ink to print; enough cash to pay the postage and keep the lights on; enough people to do the work.

They were not rich, and savings were nonexistent, but they were always supplied.

World War I

Then the whole world changed. From 1914 to 1918, boys and men from 17 to 50 were called from all over America to go to Europe and fight "the war to end all wars." Charles was over the age limit, but his son Rickert was called into duty, and went, along with millions of others, onto ships and into the battlefields of Europe.

One of the new Unity teachers wrote a prayer for the men to keep in their helmets or pockets:

> The Light of God surrounds me;
>
> The Love of God enfolds me;
>
> The Power of God protects me;
>
> The Presence of God watches over me;
>
> Wherever I am, God is.[2]

So a whole new level of prayer was called for: that these young men, and all the men called to fight in this great war, would be held in the safe and loving arms of God.

Each Unity center around the country made it a point to hold prayer vigils for the soldiers and sailors from their community.

They would see the young men in the light of God, in the safe protection of God, and returning home well and strong. They would *feel* them coming home and embracing friends and family, having safely moved through whatever apparent dangers surrounded them.

And the results were miraculous. In town after town, as World War I came to a close, men would return unscratched, or slightly wounded, telling tales of how some unlikely event had saved them, or some guiding light had led them to safety.

And among those men was Charles' son, Rickert, who, having seen the power of God amidst the nightmare of battle and the glories of Europe, was

---

[2] Written by James Dillett Freeman for Unity.

ready to do whatever he could to make the truths of Unity available to the world.

The Farm

Rickert, who was now known as "Rick," had a dream of a possibility. He saw a European-style village in which students of Unity could live, work, and study in beauty and peace. He scoured the ads and traveled far and wide across the countryside in search of the perfect property. After weeks of searching, he finally found a farm outside of Lee's Summit, an hour or so from Kansas City. It was a lovely setting, with woods, an orchard, and a creek.

He began at once to build his vision. Whenever funds could be spared and willing workers were available, he would install one more element in his dream.

First was a "cabin" for his parents, a lovely small home (without a kitchen, at Myrtle's insistence!) with a pretty porch with arches. Here they could retreat from the constant pressure of the organization that surrounded them in the city. They took their meals with others and used their space as a retreat from the world.

Then came the vegetable gardens to supply the Unity Inn—the in-house cafeteria that was becoming famous for its inexpensive, delicious vegetarian food. Rick designed them to be beautiful as well as practical, and made sure the orchards were maintained, as well.

One year, blight hit the nut trees across the Mississippi valley, and many of the trees on The

Farm had to be cut down. Rick, after talking it over with his father, acquired a sawmill and turned those dying trees into lumber for future building projects.

Then, in a stroke of genius, Rick created a water storage system that included a large pond and a tank in a tall tower—which was built like an Italian bell tower, and which also would house the offices of Silent Unity, whose continuously burning lights would be a beacon for the surrounding countryside.

The pond has inspired thousands with its peaceful beauty and the tower remains the symbol for Unity Village today.

Other buildings, open spaces, and walkways were added as the years went by. They were reminiscent of monasteries and villages in the Italian countryside, with arches over covered walkways and tile roofs that were both practical—providing lasting protection from the severe weather of the region—and beautiful.

It took decades and the efforts and imagination of many people, but by the 1930s The Farm had become Unity Village, a beautiful place where people could live, work, and study together. And Charles and Myrtle, who had been commuting between the "cabin" on The Farm and their apartment in the Unity buildings in Kansas City, could be there full time.

Heaven on Earth

While Rick was developing Unity Village, Lowell was becoming the manager of Unity Press.

Lowell had started in the same way his father had, as a boy helping load and carry the type from the editing room to the printing press. Then, as he grew, and his skills grew, he was given more responsibility and authority. Soon he was printing books and magazines by the thousands, and in time, became editor as well as printer.

Both boys benefited from their father's empowering management style. When he saw that someone had the skill to do a job, he got out of the way, letting them find their own rhythm and method. After that, he remained available to assist and provide whatever kind of back-up might be called for without getting in the way of people's learning and management processes.

In this way, Charles set up that rare sort of institution: in which no one is the only authority, but everyone is empowered to do the best they are able. Charles and Myrtle had found a way of guiding rather than managing, of leading rather than directing, that became a hallmark of the Unity movement for decades to come.

They came to this, in large part, by studying Jesus' teachings and actions as described in the Gospels. In fact, Charles came to call the Kansas City center "The Unity Society of Practical Christianity," and later incorporated it as such. Whenever he opened a meeting of other ministers and leaders in the Society, he would say, "This is the school of Jesus Christ," or among Silent Unity workers he would say, "Jesus Christ is the head of Silent Unity."

Charles had come a long way from that "mess of contradictions" he had worked through during those months after Myrtle's healing. Through his own study and with the help of Mrs. Hopkins' twelve lessons, he had come to understand the role of Jesus as the teacher, guide, and way for any of us to, as Jesus said, "do these things and greater."

He had analyzed the Greek and Hebrew words in the Old and New Testaments and come to understand those books as the story of the soul's journey to the Throne of God. He had accepted that Jesus' teachings, and the love that Jesus encouraged and inspired, were the highest and best means to experience the one power and one presence that we call God working in our lives and world.

So Charles and Myrtle, their sons and their sons' families, and the hundreds of people who worked with and for Unity, lived on a farm in Missouri, where they grew most of their food, prayed for thousands daily, and saw God's "will be done on Earth as it is in Heaven."

VII. Endings & New Beginnings

March 29, 1931 was Charles and Myrtle's 50th wedding anniversary, and a lovely ceremony was held in the chapel of the center they had build in Kansas City.

Not that anyone looking at Charles would believe that this was a man who'd been married that many years! He had begun, soon after his 50th birthday, to undo the effects of years of constant activity and little sleep. In deep meditation he had commanded his muscles to become strong and his skin to become firm, and over the next several months he had restored his body to a much younger appearance and energy level.

Charles knew that the body, being part of the omnipresent spirit we call God, was not really subject to age and its deterioration. He knew that divine energy, being the only power anywhere, was available to anyone who called upon it, at any time. So he called upon that energy to express itself in and as his body, that he might better fulfill his commitment to bring Unity and Practical Christianity into the world.

Myrtle, however, felt differently. She saw the work that she had accomplished, and all that the wonderful people around her were continuing, and decided that "it would be easier to do the work that is ahead of me from the invisible plane." She started telling their secretary, Cora Dedrick, what was needed so that all her paperwork was in order, and arranged to complete the many details that might otherwise remain undone.

Then, on the last Wednesday and Thursday of September, 1931, Myrtle worked in the Kansas City offices and led the healing meditation. The next day, Friday, she went to The Farm and headed out to the orchard to pick a few apples, using the ladders provided to get the ones in the high branches. Over the weekend, she took to her bed, and on Tuesday, October 6, she quietly slipped away, leaving her body for that "invisible plane."

At her memorial service, two weeks later, Charles said,

> "... I am constrained to speak a few words of consolation and comfort, not only for you but for myself... We who are following Jesus Christ in the resurrection know life as a spiritual thing, that we live spiritually ... and that we shall continue to live in Spirit ... And we know that this spiritual bond is the only bond that will really endure..."

She had been the love and the inspiration of his life. For fifty-five years his heart had been hers and they, together, had borne not just children and grandchildren, but a movement that was touching the lives of millions. No one could ever take her place.

Keeping At It

Yet there was much work yet to be done! There were ideas yet to be explored and presented to the world, and new technologies to understand and use!

And there were more articles for the magazine, more books in the works, more letters to write and appointments to keep.

Charles' great reference work, *The Metaphysical Bible Dictionary* came out that same year. It was the basis for much of his teaching: his explanation of all the personal and place names used in the Old and New Testaments, along with many other key words and phrases. But rather than simply defining them, Charles managed to interpret them in terms of the metaphor, or inner meaning, for the person on a spiritual journey. It was a monumental work that has been invaluable for students of Unity ever since.

That year Charles worked on another book, as well—an important contribution to the Depression era that he called *Prosperity*. Having lived through and prospered in good times and bad, he had much to say on the subject that was both useful and inspiring.

But mostly, he wanted people to understand that God, being omnipresent, was in everything. That what physicists had once called "the ether" and now were beginning to call "the quantum field" was, in fact, God's spiritual substance, everywhere and in all things, waiting for us to call it forth, through our faith, into whatever form our hearts desire.

This was an amazing new message in those days—and an important one to remember today, as well.

A New Partnership

Charles was aware that the women in his life had been invaluable in helping him achieve his goals. First of all, his mother, whose tireless support during those years of illness as a child had kept him alive, had continued to be supportive through his adult years as the main housekeeper for his family. Then there was that neighbor lady who had tutored him and shown him the possibilities of a much larger world than St. Cloud, Minnesota, when he was a teen. Then, of course, his beloved Myrtle, whose deep spiritual life had always inspired and motivated him and whose wisdom had been part of his guidance system all these years.

Now, he realized, the pattern was continuing. He saw that their faithful secretary, Cora, was taking on that supportive role. She had been helping with his and Myrtle's personal and professional work for over a decade, and did so as much out of love for them as for appreciation of their ideas and any financial support she received.

Not only did she handle all their correspondence, she managed their files and manuscripts, made sure appointments were scheduled and met, and handled the logistics of all their trips between Unity Village and Kansas City. She participated in many of their prayer circles and was a major contributor in their classes, as well. Then, when Myrtle passed on, she took on the minor details of life, like making sure Charles' laundry and mending were handled and that the linens at "the Cabin" and in the apartment in the city were kept fresh.

So nobody was too surprised when, a few years after Myrtle passed on, Charles and Cora were quietly married.

People were amazed, however, when soon after that, Charles resigned as head of the Unity organization—until they understood that it was to free him to travel and take the Unity message to other places in the country.

So Charles, now almost 80 years old, rode the trains again, and this time went far beyond the mountains of Colorado to the far-away shores of the Atlantic and Pacific oceans. And Cora made it easy for him to do so.

A New Home

At first, they kept a "home base" just outside of Unity village. Charles had arranged for a lovely, Southern style home to be built at "Unity Ridge" on property that Cora owned. It had high ceilings and a deep front porch where several people could visit on a pleasant afternoon.

Soon, however, it became clear that if Charles were around, others would not take the authority that was theirs to run the organization.

And, besides, he had seen on his train trips across country that there was warm sunshine and a lot of wonderful things happening in and around Los Angeles!

So Charles bought a little house in the San Fernando Valley, north of Los Angeles proper.

Now, at that time, "the Valley" was full of farms and beautiful orange groves with few roads—not anything like the network of freeways and suburbs that it is today. And Charles, approaching 90 years old, really appreciated the freedom to be outdoors, the warmth of the sun—and the reception he received from his audiences.

Thousands of people would come to hear him speak, in halls and churches all around the area. They loved his "down home" style and easy way of presenting his ideas. And they deeply appreciated Cora's prayers and meditations.

He enjoyed being part of the broadcasting and film industry that were emerging in those days, as well. He continued to do radio broadcasts and made some recordings while he was there.

And he truly enjoyed watching movies about the old Wild West! Was he reliving those early days in Texas and Colorado on the movie screen?

Each summer, he and Cora would return to Unity Village, where he would teach a few classes, advise a few students, and spend time with family and friends. His grandchildren loved to be with him — he never preached; just was warm, friendly, and kind. And sometimes, when they were hurting, he'd just sit with them until they fell asleep; then, when they woke up, they felt better.

New Insights & Understandings

Charles continued to study and wrote a few books during those years, always discovering new insights and new ways of expressing the fundamental truths that he lived by. He was committed to finding ways to get everybody to see that if they would only allow themselves to be in unity with the divine, the divine would work to accomplish great things for them!

One of those books was called *The Atom-smashing Power of the Mind.* When Charles learned that Enrico Fermi and his team at the University of Chicago had managed to split the atom, he was fascinated! So much power in such a tiny thing! It was the perfect metaphor for explaining God's ever-present power to work good in our lives — and the role of our thoughts in bringing that about.

Another book, *Teach Us to Pray*, was printed in 1941, and both Charles and Cora are listed as the authors. Unlike Charles' other books, in which he develops an idea, this one is a collection of short

pieces—mostly from Charles' talks—designed to
reassure and inspire the reader. In it, they remind us
that when we invoke "God with us" or Emanuel
(which is the Hebrew word for that idea) with the
name Jesus Christ, we are calling forth the same Life
and Power in us—just as Christ taught in the gospels.

Moving On

During World War II, Charles and Cora went all
over the country, meeting people and giving them
strength and hope. And Charles kept finding new
ways to explain the ideas of Unity. Cora worked
quietly in the background, keeping everything
running smoothly, while Charles took center stage.
People loved and appreciated them both and they
were both doing the work they loved.

Charles continued his daily periods "in the
silence," morning and evening, as well as teaching
and leading prayer circles. When he was at home, he
continued his pattern of working far into the night
and "cat-napping" during the day. On the road,
though, he would reverse that pattern, going "early
to bed and early to rise" so he wouldn't miss
anything that might be seen during daylight hours.

From his early studies, and as he continued his
prayer time, Charles came to believe that each of us
has, as the apostle Paul had hoped, the potential to
join in Jesus' resurrection. He even wondered if the
body couldn't be immortal—if proper diet, exercise,
and spiritual practice couldn't overcome the effects of
aging.

Certainly, to look at him, one could believe it! In
1946, just before his 92nd birthday, he looked like a

man in his 70s and had a travel, teaching, and publishing schedule that a much younger man would find tiring. During that time, he wrote a note saying "I fairly sizzle with zeal and enthusiasm!"

He was living life to the fullest, expressing the Holy Spirit, or Christ nature, as completely as possible, and he understood that Jesus expected us all to be able to "overcome death."

The winter of 1947 was spent, as usual, at their home in California. Charles spoke to several large audiences and taught classes, as well as continuing to write.

Then, in February of 1948, he didn't feel well (some sources say pneumonia was the culprit), so Cora persuaded him to cancel the rest of his spring schedule. Over the next several weeks, for the first time since he was a child, Charles spent most of his time in bed, sleeping.

By April, Charles' family was concerned and persuaded him to come home to Unity Farm. Cora once more arranged everything for a smooth journey and Charles was soon established in his old bed in their home.

There, people would come and visit, share stories, and tell jokes, just to see him smile. He said little, but clearly enjoyed their visits. Several times during the day, Cora would read to him—often his own writings—helping keep his mind focused on what he considered most important: "divine love."

As spring moved into summer, it became clear to all that Charles was not going to recover. At the end of June, he said, "It looks like I'll have to go, but don't worry, I'll be back…I am going to have a new body, anyway, and this time it's going to be a perfect body!"

On the 4ᵗʰ of July, he sat up and said, "Don't you see it? The New Jerusalem, coming down from God: the new heaven and new earth!"

And on the morning of the 5ᵗʰ, he awoke, saw his son Lowell standing beside him, smiled, and was gone.

Today, millions of people continue to read his books and *The Daily Word,* and hundreds of thousands attend classes, prayer circles, and Sunday services based on the wisdom that Charles Fillmore discovered and shared.

The Power of Unity with Divine Good is awesome indeed!

About the Author

Ruth L. Miller is a minister who has written several books about the history of what is called "New Thought" or "metaphysical" religion in America. Her first book, *150 Years of Healing* is an introduction to the founders and leaders of the New Thought movement. Her *Unveiling Your Hidden Power* explains the teachings of Emma Curtis Hopkins, and is available as a text, a workbook, and a guide for teachers. *A Power Beyond Magic* is a biography of Ernest Holmes for youth.

Dr. Miller earned degrees in anthropology, cybernetics, environmental studies, and systems science, then worked as a futurist and professor before preparing for ordination as a minister. In the process, she raised two daughters, one of whom is now a doctor and the other is a media producer. She now serves Unity and Religious Science centers in Oregon.

About the Illustrator

Martha Shonkwiler is a retired school teacher, perpetual student, and a grandmother. After a career as a teacher, she studied "Healing through Art and Spirituality," receiving three theological seminary and university degrees. Then she volunteered for six years as a chaplain, labyrinth facilitator, art therapist and "Healing Touch" practitioner at the hospital in Grants Pass, Oregon, where she lives in the beautiful woods.

Her focus now is relaxing, creating art, and enjoying her grandchildren (and children) with nature walks, art, and travel adventures. Martha appreciates the Grants Pass Center for Spiritual Living.

by Emma Curtis Hopkins

Resume

High Mysticism

Scientific Christian Mental Practice

The Gospel Series

Esoteric Philosophy

Class Lessons of 1888

The Judgment Series in Spiritual Science

Self Treatments

Drops of Gold

Bible Interpretation Series 1–22

by Ruth L. Miller

Unveiling Your Hidden Power: Emma Curtis Hopkins'
Metaphysics for the 21st Century

The Power of Unity – Charles Fillmore biography

A Power Beyond Magic – Ernest Holmes Biography

The Power of Mind – Phineas P. Quimby Biography

The Power of Insight – Thomas Troward Biography

The Power of the Self – Ralph Waldow Emerson Bio

The Power of Practice – Emily Cady Biography

Power to Heal Emma Curtis – Hopkins Biography

Available at www.wisewomanpress.com

Paths of Power

Boys and girls and men and women all over the world have found a kind of power that transforms lives. These are their stories—how they found the power, what they did with it, and how their own lives were transformed in the process.

This kind of power is greater than magic, because it transforms, not just changing appearances. And it is, as the great teacher Emma Hopkins said, "more than supernatural; it is supremely natural."

The *Paths of Power* series tells the stories of those who've gone before so that new generations will discover and use these remarkably human, God-given abilities.

www.ingramcontent.com/pod-product-compliance
Lightning Source LLC
Chambersburg PA
CBHW081523040426
42447CB00013B/3323